PROJECT

CODE

CREATE YOUR OWN STORY WITH SCRATCH

Kevin Wood

Illustrated by
Glen McBeth

W
FRANKLIN WATTS
LONDON • SYDNEY

Franklin Watts
First published in Great Britain in 2017 by
The Watts Publishing Group

Credits
Series Editor: Julia Adams/Julia Bird
Series Designer: Alix Wood
Cover Designer: Peter Scoulding
Illustrations: Glen McBeth

Speech bubble designed by Freepik

ISBN: 978 1 4451 5642 2

Printed in China

MIX
Paper from
responsible sources
FSC® C104740
FSC
www.fsc.org

Franklin Watts
An imprint of
Hachette Children's Group
Part of The Watts Publishing Group
Carmelite House
50 Victoria Embankment
London EC4Y 0DZ

An Hachette UK Company
www.hachette.co.uk

www.franklinwatts.co.uk

Using Scratch

Scratch is a programming language designed by MIT (Massachusetts Institute of Technology) that lets you create your own interactive stories, animations, games, music and art. Rather than using a complex computer language, it uses easy-to-understand coding blocks. To get the most out of this book, you will need to be able to use a computer and you will need to load Scratch onto your computer. Always check with an adult if it is OK to download files from the Internet to your computer. Go to: **https://scratch.mit.edu**

First, do Scratch's 'Getting Started with Scratch' tutorial, found by going to 'Create' on the home page, and then look in the 'Tips' menu. You can also work on Scratch offline. Scroll to the bottom of the homepage and click on Offline Editor in the Support menu. Follow the instructions to install it on your computer.

CONTENTS

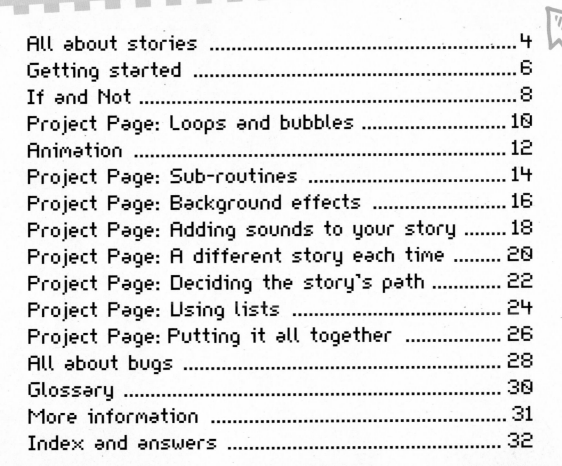

To load the projects that you will use in this book, go to:

www.alixwoodbooks.co.uk/projectcode/downloads.php

and select 'Story'. Save the folder somewhere on your computer where you will be able to find it again. You will need to open files in this folder as you go through the project.

Every effort has been made by the Publishers to ensure that the websites in this book are suitable for children, that they are of the highest educational value, and that they contain no inappropriate or offensive material. However, because of the nature of the Internet, it is impossible to guarantee that the contents of these sites will not be altered. We strongly advise that Internet access is supervised by a responsible adult.

Words in **bold** are in the glossary on page 30.

ALL ABOUT STORIES

>>> Do you like stories? You have probably read a lot of them at home and at school. Do you have a favourite story? Why do you like it so much?

A good story usually has ...

- strong **characters**: these are the people or animals that the story is about. If your story is about the adventures of a family of rabbits, for example, the rabbits are the characters. The main character in a story works best if the reader cares about what happens to them.

- a **plot**: the plot usually involves something that the main character has to work through, such as a problem. Often the problem gets very complicated, and then gets solved at the end of the story.

- a **setting**: the setting is where the story takes place, such as in a forest, or at some time in history.

4

Types of book

Most of the stories you have read are probably in books. Books are the way we have shared stories for hundreds of years. We can buy or borrow books, pass them on to our friends and read them anywhere. Nowadays, books can also be read on-screen, using a **computer** (for example an e-reader, a smartphone or a tablet). These books are called **e-books**, which is short for 'electronic books'. The story in an e-book is often the same as in the printed version, with the same pictures and words.

Think about it

You can listen to stories as an audiobook. An audiobook is a recording of actors reading the story out loud. Audiobooks can also feature music, and the character's voices. What is missing from an audiobook, though?

(The answers are on page 32.)

Stories from Scratch

You can write your own stories using the computer program Scratch. You can create **animations** that help to tell your story. Using **code**, you can tell the computer how to show the words and pictures of your story. You can even add sounds!

Once you have coded your story, click on the play button (green flag) and watch your story come to life!

GETTING STARTED

To create a story in Scratch, we need to start by writing the words that make up the story (known as the text). We can set words against a background to make the story look more interesting. You can choose a background you like from the Scratch library, or even make your own. You will need to be careful that the background isn't too dark, or too busy, so that it's still possible to read the text. The words can be added directly on to the background, or set into a **sprite** (character).

Open project Story 1a in Scratch. This is the beginning of a story about a boy in a forest who hears a strange noise.

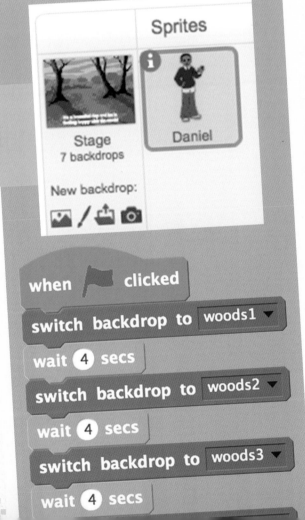

The story is written in short parts that sit on separate background slides. The picture in each background slide is the same, it's just the text that changes. Each background slide acts like a page. When you click on the flag, the code starts moving through each 'page', showing each one for four seconds. The code looks like this:

6

AHA!

As you can see, the code is quite long and a lot of it is repeated There is a neater way to write code like this — you can write it in a **loop. Programmers** use loops to tell the computer to repeat a set of instructions. In Scratch, you can create a loop to:
- repeat the code a number of times
- repeat the code forever
- repeat the code until something else happens.

Creating loops in Scratch

To create a loop in Scratch, you use the 'Forever', 'Repeat' or 'Repeat until' blocks.

Open Story 1b in Scratch. Look at the new loop we have created. It makes the code much shorter and easier to read. The 'Repeat' bracket tells the computer to run the code inside it six times, every four seconds.

```
when [flag] clicked
switch backdrop to woods1 ▾
repeat 6
    wait 4 secs
    switch backdrop to next backdrop ▾
```

IF AND NOT

What did you think about the way the pages turned? Did they move faster than you wanted? Did you miss any of the story? Or were the pages too slow? Maybe it would be better to have the reader control when they want to see the next page.

Moving through the story

Open Story 1c in Scratch. This project tells the next part of the story. It includes two arrow sprites, placed in the bottom corners of the screen. If you click on the right arrow, you move to the next page. The left arrow takes you back a page, in case you missed something. There is also code that moves you to the next page when you press the spacebar. Click on the Daniel sprite to see the code in our program.

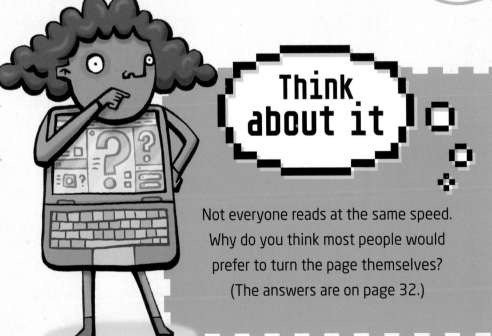

Think about it

Not everyone reads at the same speed. Why do you think most people would prefer to turn the page themselves?

(The answers are on page 32.)

8

Did you spot a bug?

Have you noticed that if you keep clicking the right arrow and moving the story forwards, you end up going back to the start and repeating the story? If this is something you think shouldn't happen, it is a coding error, or **bug**. Let's look at the next project to see how this bug can be fixed.

>>> Open Story 1d in Scratch. The code now looks like this:

The added code tells the computer to only switch to the next backdrop IF the current backdrop is NOT called 'woods7'. So once the backdrop 'woods 7' is showing (the last page of the story), this piece of code stops the loop turning to the next page.

```
when  space ▾  key pressed
if      not       backdrop name   =  woods7      then
    switch backdrop to  next backdrop ▾
```

Using IF helps your code make decisions. Each time the loop code displays a new backdrop, it will ask IF the current backdrop is NOT called 'woods7'. As long as that statement is true, and the backdrop is not called 'woods7', the code will change the backdrop to the next one. When that statement is false, and 'wood7' is the backdrop, then the code will stop looping.

TRUE   FALSE

LOOPS AND BUBBLES

Up until now, we have coded our story to display (show) a bit like a book — page by page. Another way to display the text of a story is to have it scrolling on the screen. You may have seen this used in movies, too.

Open Story 1e in Scratch. When you click the flag, the text now rolls from the bottom of the screen to the top, waiting for two seconds before each new line is displayed. In this code, the story is set in a sprite, called Story, instead of on the backdrop.

The Story code looks like this.

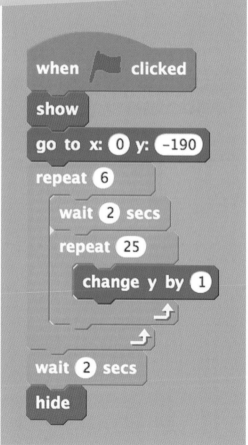

```
when 🏳 clicked
show
go to x: 0 y: -190
repeat 6
    wait 2 secs
    repeat 25
        change y by 1
wait 2 secs
hide
```

In this program, you can see the story code if you click on the story sprite.

Sprites

Stage
1 backdrop

Daniel

Story

New backdrop:

AHA!

Loops inside loops

We use two loops here, one inside the other. When one loop is inside another we call this a **nested loop**. The outer loop is run once for each time the story moves a line up the screen. The inside loop shows each new line of the story on the screen. Once the entire story has been shown, and we have given the reader time to read it, the story is hidden.

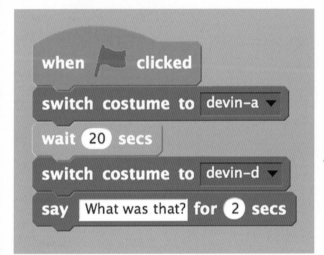

```
when [flag] clicked
switch costume to devin-a ▼
wait 20 secs
switch costume to devin-d ▼
say What was that? for 2 secs
```

Scratch uses speech and thought bubbles to show who is thinking or speaking. We use a speech bubble at the end of the story to show Daniel is talking. Daniel changes **costume** to look as if he is speaking, too. Costumes are the same sprite drawn in different poses.

 The Daniel sprite code looks like this.

The code just waits long enough for the entire story to be shown and then hidden. Then we make Daniel speak his line.

To make a sprite speak, go to the Looks menu. Find this block:

```
say Hello! for 2 secs
```

Type what you want the sprite to say in the white area where it says 'Hello!'

Hello!

ANIMATION

>>> Let's start a new story. Chrissie is looking for her puppy. As this story is about a character travelling between different places, it would be great if Chrissie walked on and off the screen each time. >>>

When we make a character move on screen, it is called animation. Open Story 2a in Scratch. Click on the flag to read the first part of the story.

AHA!

We make Chrissie look as if she is walking by showing different pictures of her, one after the other. Each picture shows her in a slightly different walking pose. The images change so quickly that this makes it look like Chrissie is actually moving. She is animated!

Coding unplugged

How can still images look as if they are moving? Draw a puppy in the centre of a circle of card. Draw a dog bed on the other side. Punch a hole in either side of the card circle and thread a rubber band through each hole. Now hold a rubber band in each hand and roll them between your thumb and forefinger to spin the card. As the disc spins, your eyes should see the two drawings become one image. This is how animation works, by tricking your eyes into merging fast-moving images.

Chrissie reacts in a few ways during the story. She reacts when her puppy has an accident; we code this by changing her costume. Some Scratch sprites have different costumes that make them change their expression, or move their arms or legs. To make Chrissie look like she is walking in Scratch we use different costumes, too. Chrissie's code looks like this:

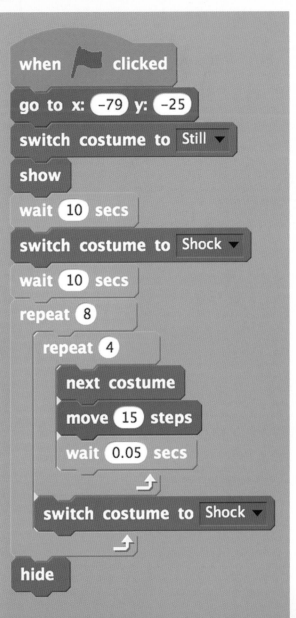

PROJECT PAGE:
SUB-ROUTINES

As the story continues, Chrissie will be walking to a few different places. We don't really want to have to repeat the same code each time. Instead, we can use a **sub-routine**.

AHA!

Sub-routines are great if you want to repeat a piece of code. First, you write the piece of code and give it a name, for example 'Walking'. Now, every time you want to use 'Walking', you just have to call for it by name in your code and your program will run it. The 'Walking' code is called a sub-routine.

Using blocks

1 In Scratch, you can make a new block to create a sub-routine. Simply click the 'More Blocks' tab and select 'Make a Block'. Type the name of your sub-routine into the block.

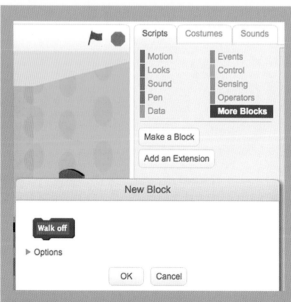

2 Once you have given your block a name, you should see the 'define' block appear. Snap the blocks that you need for your sub-routine to the bottom of your 'Define' block.

3 Scratch stores your sub-routine, ready for you to use any time you want. Here, we have called one of our new blocks 'Walk off' and written its code.

4 Any new sub-routine blocks will appear when you click on the sprite that you wrote them for. Open Story 2b in Scratch. Click on Chrissie and 'More Blocks' and you will see them appear under the 'Make a Block' button.

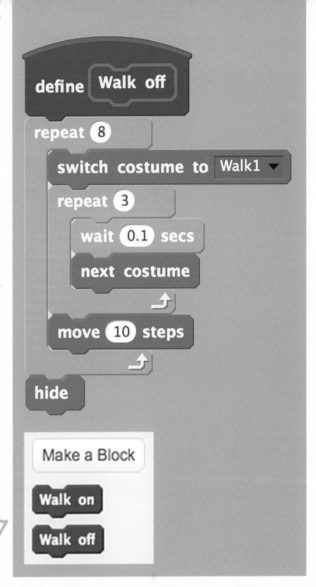

Speedy shortcut

Now when we want to run that walking loop, we can just use the sub-routine instead of writing it all out again.

>>> Have a look at how sub-routines work as the story continues. Still in Story 2b in Scratch, click on the flag to read the next part of our lost puppy story. >>>

BACKGROUND EFFECTS

>>> Our coded story is taking shape! So far, we have a main character and she can walk and move between scenes. Let's see which other elements we can add to our story by using animation.

At the moment, we have different settings in our story, but the backgrounds are a little dull. We can make them more interesting by adding animated elements that help set the scene.

Open Story 2c in Scratch. Click on the flag to read the next part of the story.

Think about it

Did you notice the butterflies in the background? Instead of just describing them, a Scratch animation can bring the scene to life. What other details could you add to your story to make it come alive?

1 We added some little butterflies using **cloning blocks**. A clone is a copy. A clone of a sprite is exactly the same as the 'parent' sprite. You can change a clone a little bit, though. In this story, we have made the clone butterflies slightly smaller. To make a clone, first click on the butterfly sprite. Then go to 'Control' and choose the cloning block 'Create clone of (myself)'.

create clone of myself ▼

2 If you leave the menu selection as 'myself' it means that the sprite selected will be cloned. You can choose how many clones you want. Then use a 'When I start as a clone' block to give the clones their own code instructions. We have made the clone butterflies fly around.

```
when I start as a clone
set size to 10 %
repeat until  backdrop name = Park
    repeat 4
        next costume
        wait 0.1 secs
    glide 0.25 secs to x: pick random -240 to 240 y: pick random -36 to 180
delete this clone
```

Fluttering here and there

We want the butterflies to fly about in a **random** way. We do this by using two 'Pick random ( ) to ( )' blocks, set in a 'Glide ( ) secs to x: ( ) y: ( )' block. You can enter a value in each space of the 'Pick random' blocks. This sets the range from which each block randomly chooses a value. The 'x' and 'y' values are called **coordinates**. They help us locate a point on our screen. The 'x' tells us how far along the width of the screen this point is; the 'y' value tells us how high up it is. In our example, we have set 'y' as -240 to 240. This is the whole screen left to right, so we are telling the block to choose any spot along the width of the screen. We have programmed the x value to be any number between -36 and 180, which is the height of the area where the flowers are on the screen. The butterflies will only fly around the flowers now.

ADDING SOUNDS TO YOUR STORY

>>> Now we have made the backgrounds more fun to look at. let's add something else that can really bring a story to life: sound! >>>

While printed stories can be great at describing sounds, they can never actually play them. But one of the exciting things about creating a story in Scratch is that you can add sound effects! For example, when Chrissie is in the garden, maybe we could hear some birds singing, or wind rustling through the trees?
Let's explore how we can add sounds to our story.

>>> Open Story 2d in Scratch. Click on the flag to read the last part of the story. >>>

You can find sounds to use in Scratch's Sound Library. If you can't find the sound you want, you can import a sound from your computer, or you can even record your own sound.

Chirp!

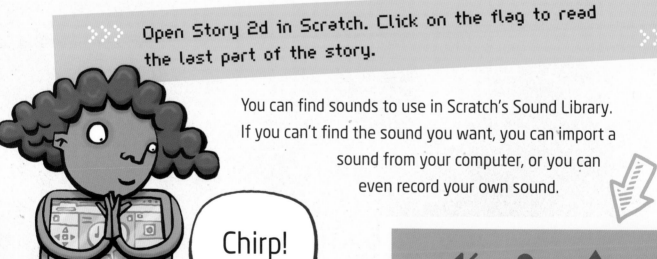

use library sound	record sound	import sound

We couldn't find the sound we wanted in Scratch's Sound Library. We had a sound file on our computer that we wanted to use instead, so we clicked on the file icon and selected our file. The code for the imported sound looks like this:

play sound Dragon Roaring.mp3 ▾ until done

Think about it

Did you think the roar of the dragon made the story come to life? What sound did Chrissie hear that might have made her feel happy in the story?

(The answers are on page 32.)

Picking your sound effects

Have a look at the Sound Library to discover some of the sound effects that you could use for your story. You could use sounds such as music or birds tweeting as background noise. You might also want to add speech to your story. Scratch has some other really cool noises, too. Try clicking on the electronic space ripple noise or the computer beeps. Maybe you could use them if one of your characters was a robot?

Sound Library

Category
All
Animal
Effects
Electronic
Human
Instruments
Music Loops
Musical Notes

bird   chee chee   chomp   cricket   crickets

dog2   duck   goose   horse gallop   horse

PROJECT PAGE:
A DIFFERENT STORY EACH TIME

>>> So far, our story has stayed the same each time we have read it. That's pretty normal for a story printed on paper, but one of the great things about Scratch is that we can make our story a little bit different each time! >>>

Open Story 3 in Scratch. When you click the flag, you will see our character Giga looking for her friend, Pico, to play with. Eventually, she finds him. But each time you click the flag, the story changes, and she finds him in a different place. The code block used for this is called 'Pick random'.

1 The story has four backgrounds, called Background1, Background2, Background3 and Background4. We need the block to choose one, at random, for Pico to wait in.

This is the piece of the code that makes the story random:

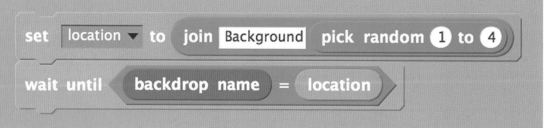

```
set  location ▼  to  join  Background  pick random 1 to 4

wait until  backdrop name  =  location
```

2   We ask the code to choose a number between 1 and 4. It adds that number to the end of the word 'Background' and stores the result in a **variable** (see below) called 'Location'. Once the code has picked its random location, the Pico code waits until this backdrop comes around in the story. When the background in the story matches the 'Location' background, Pico's code makes him appear.

3   The Giga code walks through each location, calling for Pico. Her code repeats this loop until the backdrop name is the same as the variable 'Location'. This is where she will find Pico. They walk off together and the story ends.

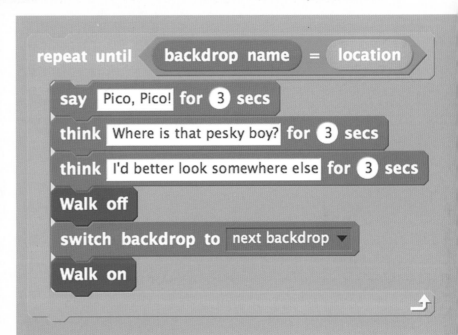

```
repeat until     backdrop name   =   location
    say   Pico, Pico!  for  3  secs
    think   Where is that pesky boy?  for  3  secs
    think   I'd better look somewhere else  for  3  secs
    Walk  off
    switch  backdrop  to   next backdrop  ▼
    Walk  on
```

What is a variable?
Data that may need to change is known as a variable. Variables can be numbers or words. Think of a variable as being a little like a container for data. You give your variable a name and then store data in it. You can use that data at any time. When you type the variable's name, your code will fetch the data that you put in that box.

PROJECT PAGE:
DECIDING THE STORY'S PATH

>>> Probably the best thing about creating a story on a computer is that you can make it **interactive**. That means what happens in the story can be changed by the reader. A story could have many different endings depending on the options chosen as you read it. >>>

Open Story 4a in Scratch. Click the green flag to start the story. In the text you will be asked questions. Press the '1' or '2' key on your keyboard to select your answer. Keep selecting answers until the end of the story. Did you save Princess Ruby? Try running the story again and choose different options.

Creating this story involved a lot of code, but the most important bit is the sub-routine called 'Question'. This allows us to interact with the story. Click on the Ruby sprite's code. You can see that the 'Question' sub-routine waits for the story to be told by the different backdrops with the text on them. Then it asks the user the question 'What should I do?' The user presses key '1' or '2'.

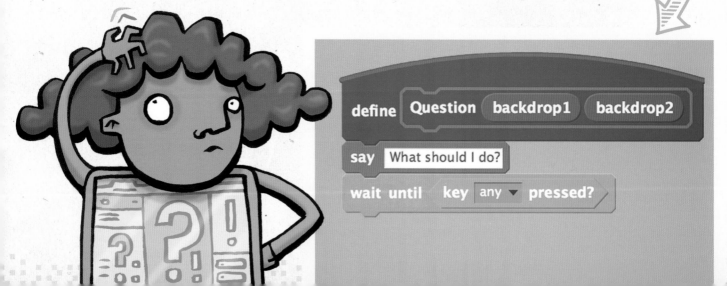

If you look back at the main code, you will see that two backdrop names are entered into the 'Question' code block. If key 1 is pressed, the first backdrop appears. If key 2 is pressed, we see the second backdrop.

If the backdrop has 'end' in its name, it means Ruby is taken prisoner. Any other backdrops move the reader to the next scene.

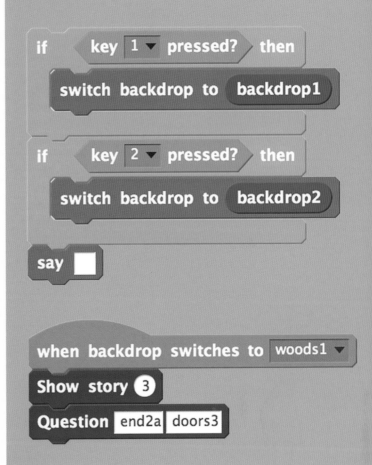

```
if      key  1 ▼  pressed?   then
        switch backdrop to   backdrop1

if      key  2 ▼  pressed?   then
        switch backdrop to   backdrop2

say  ▢

when backdrop switches to  woods1 ▼
Show story 3
Question  end2a  doors3
```

When this happens, do that
Most of this code is event-driven. That is, the code looks for something to happen and then reacts to it. In this case, each sprite is looking for the backdrop belonging to the part of the story that they are involved in. They do this using the code "When backdrop switches to". Once they see the backdrop that they are waiting for, this event causes them to run their piece of the code.

AHA!

PROJECT PAGE:
USING LISTS

In the Princess Ruby story, you had to make many choices, and each one affected her journey. Hopefully, you eventually managed to get her safely back to her father's castle. Do you remember each choice you made to save her?

Think about it

What were you thinking each time Ruby was put in jail? Were you trying to remember all your choices, and where you might have gone wrong? What if we could end the story with Ruby thinking about each choice she made, and whether it was the right one? That way, it would be easier to go back to the beginning and make the right choice to keep her out of jail.

Try it

Open Story 4b in Scratch. Now, if Ruby gets captured, she thinks through every choice that was made on her journey. This is done using a special variable called a **list**. A list, as its name suggests, allows you to store a list of things. In this case it is the list of choices that you made in the story. We have called this list 'Choices' and it is used each time the princess ends up in jail.

What should I do?

1 Right at the start of the code, we clear the list, so that it is empty.

```
delete  all ▼  of  Choices ▼
```

2 Next, in the 'Question' block, we add a value to the list each time a question is answered. As there are always two answer choices, we either add a '1' or a '2'.

```
add  1  to  Choices ▼

add  2  to  Choices ▼
```

3 The new code at the end of the 'Go to jail' block works through the list and makes Ruby think something, based on your answers. It's a long bit of code, but it's pretty simple, really. The code asks 'If the answer was 1 or 2, Then think something, Else think something else.'

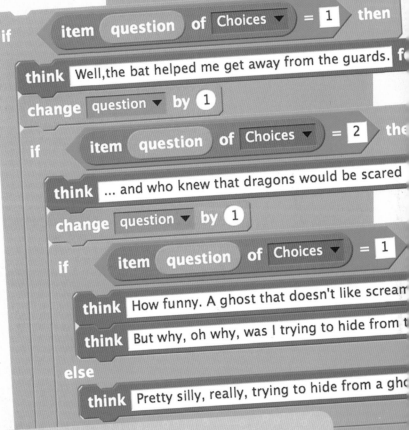

```
if   item  question  of  Choices ▼  = 1   then
  think  Well, the bat helped me get away from the guards.  f
  change  question ▼  by  1
  if   item  question  of  Choices ▼  = 2   the
    think  ... and who knew that dragons would be scared
    change  question ▼  by  1
    if   item  question  of  Choices ▼  = 1
      think  How funny. A ghost that doesn't like scream
      think  But why, oh why, was I trying to hide from t
    else
      think  Pretty silly, really, trying to hide from a gh
```

Still not a g

help me.

If, Then, Else
Asking questions such as If, Then, Else allows the code to make decisions.
For example, if Princess Ruby gives the dragon a biscuit, Then she goes to jail, Else she moves to the castle corridor.

PROJECT PAGE:
PUTTING IT ALL TOGETHER

>>> Once you have got your story and characters sorted, it's time to put everything together. The final version of our Lost Puppy story uses many of the fun story elements that we have looked at so far. There are also some extra animations and sound effects. See if you can spot them! Open Story 5 in Scratch. >>>

To start with, the code may look quite complicated, as there are 11 backdrops, 21 sprites and a number of sounds! But don't worry. It is mainly the code we have already looked at, just all together in one program.

1 We have changed Chrissie's walking code, and now use these two new sub-routines:

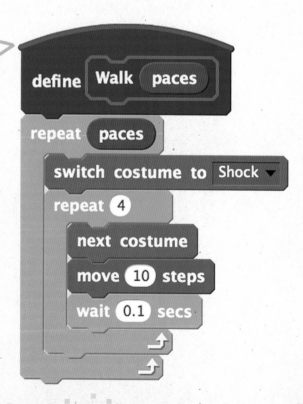

```
define Walk to (backdrop)

Walk 8
switch backdrop to (backdrop)
go to x: -244 y: -14
Walk 4
switch costume to Still ▾
```

```
define Walk (paces)

repeat (paces)
    switch costume to Shock ▾
    repeat 4
        next costume
        move 10 steps
        wait 0.1 secs
```

Now, to move from one page to another you just need to use a sub-routine block, for instance:

`Walk to house`

Chrissie now walks off to the right of the current page, the backdrop is changed to 'house' and Chrissie walks on from the left. Do you think that this makes the code easier to read?

2 It may not be obvious at first, but the road section has a random element. Each time you read the story, the piece of road will be different, and will feature a different vehicle. The random element code looks like this:

`Walk to (join road pick random 1 to 4)`
`broadcast (join Car pick random 1 to 5)`

3 There are four 'street' backdrops called road1 to road4. The block randomly chooses one of them by picking a number from 1 to 4 and adding it to the end of the word 'road'. The same happens with the word 'car', adding a random number from 1 to 5, to make a name that we **broadcast**.

Waiting for the call

Broadcasting is a way to send a message from one sprite to another. As Chrissie walks along the road, the code broadcasts a message to pick a random car to drive by.

ALL ABOUT BUGS

>>> When you write computer code, things can go wrong and errors, or bugs, can sometimes mean your code doesn't work properly. >>>

Testing, testing

There are lots of different types of bug. You need to test your code as you go along to check everything works as you planned. Things can go wrong for a number of reasons. Sometimes you may have just entered a wrong number somewhere. Other times you may have simply got your code in the wrong order.

Bug fixing

When we fix bugs, it is called **debugging**. Finding the piece of code that is wrong can be quite hard. You have to look through the code carefully. You also have to make sure that any changes you make don't create another bug! In complicated computer programs some bugs go unnoticed even when the program is finished and sold to people. That is why programs often have updates with bug fixes.

Expect the unexpected!

Sometimes someone using your code may do something that you hadn't expected. It's good to get lots of different people to test your code. The more people that play with it, the more unexpected things you can test for and fix any bugs you find.

We all make mistakes!

Don't worry if your code goes wrong, no one is perfect and it happens to the best programmers. If you wrote some code with no bugs in, first time, it must have been really simple code! When you try to write something complicated, things are bound to go wrong at first. That's good. It means you are trying something complex!

Think about it

Debugging can be troublesome! There's a sad little programmer's song that goes like this:

99 little bugs in the code
99 little bugs in the code
1 bug fixed, run the code again,
100 little bugs in the code!

Now, use the skills you have learned, and try writing some stories of your own! >>>

GLOSSARY

animation A character that moves around on screen and looks like it has come to life.

broadcast To send a message in Scratch.

bug A mistake in a computer program that means it can't run properly.

character A person in a story or play.

cloning block A tool in Scratch that allows you to make exact copies of a sprite.

code A set of instructions for a computer.

computer A programmable (usually electronic) machine that can store, retrieve, and work with data. Smartphones, tablets and laptops are all computers.

coordinates Any of a set of numbers used to locate a point on a line, a surface or a map.

costume In Scratch, costumes are the different positions each sprite is drawn in, which give the illusion of movement when they are shown one after the other.

debug To remove mistakes from a computer program.

e-book An electronic version of a printed book which can be read on a computer or an e-reader.

interactive Allowing two-way electronic communication, such as between a person and a computer.

list A way of storing data in code.

loop A series of instructions that is repeated until a condition to end is met, but may loop infinitely.

nested loop A loop within a loop.

plot The main story of a book or film.

programmer Someone who writes the code for a computer program.

random Showing no clear pattern.

setting The background, such as the time and place, of the action of a story or performance.

sprite In Scratch, a character that can be moved around within a larger scene.

sub-routine A set of instructions designed to perform a repeated operation in a program.

variable An element, feature or factor that is liable to vary or change.

MORE INFORMATION

BOOKS

Edge, Christopher. *How to Write Your Best Story Ever!* OUP, Oxford, UK: 2015.

Vorderman, Carol. *Coding With Scratch Made Easy.* DK Children, London, UK: 2015.

Wainewright, Max. *I'm an Advanced Scratch Coder (Generation Code)*, Wayland, London: 2017.

WEBSITES

MIT's Scratch website, where you can download the program for free

https://scratch.mit.edu/about/

Kids on the Net site with advice on story writing

www.kidsonthenet.org.uk/create/howtostory.htms

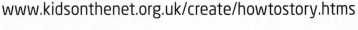

VISIT

Discover Children's Story Centre, Stratford, London. This fun, interactive museum encourages children to create their own stories.
The Story Museum, Oxford, brings some of your favourite stories to life and encourages young visitors to try their own creative writing. You can walk through a cupboard into Narnia or fall down a rabbit's hole into Wonderland!

INDEX

ANSWERS

page 5   An audiobook does not have any pictures or animation.

page 8   So they can read the story at their preferred pace.

page 19   Hearing the sound of her puppy barking.